DID ANYTHING GOOD OUT OF...

THE GREAT DEPRESSION?

EMMA MARRIOTT

WAYLAND

Published in Great Britain in 2018 by Wayland

Produced for Wayland by Tall Tree Ltd
Designers: Jonathan Vipond and Ed Simkins
Editors: Jon Richards and Joe Fullman

Dewey number: 338.5'42-dc23
ISBN 978 0 7502 9726 4

FSC

Wayland, an imprint of Hachette Children's Group
Part of Hodder and Stoughton
Carmelite House
50 Victoria Embankment
London EC4Y 0DZ

An Hachette UK Company
www.hachette.co.uk
www.hachettechildrens.co.uk

Printed and bound in China

10 9 8 7 6 5 4 3 2 1

The publisher would like to thank the following for their kind permission to reproduce their photographs:

Key: (t) top; (c) centre; (b) bottom; (l) left; (r) right

The following images are public domain: Front Cover c. Back Cover tl cl bl. Endpapers.
4–5c, 5tr br, 6tl, 6–7b, 7tr, 8tl, 9c br, 10br, 11br, 12br b, 13cr, 14br tr, 15tr b, 16c bl, 17tl b, 18tr bl,
19tl tr bl, 20tl, 21t br, 24–25c, 25tc tr, 26bl c, 27tr br, 28–29t, 29tr, 30tl, 31tr br, 34tr, 35t, 39bl cr,
40tl tr c, 41tl, 42bl, 43b, 45tr, 4b

All other images istock.com unless otherwise indicated.

13tl German Federal Archive. 20b UK National Archives, 22–23b rickpilot_2000, 23t World Trade Organization,
23cr Andrzej Barabasz, 29bl German Federal Archive, 30–31b MrX, 37tl German Federal Archive,
42c German Federal Archive, 43tl German Federal Archive, 44cl Chad Teer, 47b German Federal Archive.

CONTENTS

In October 1929, panic erupted in the New York Stock Exchange on Wall Street with investors selling millions of company stocks over a few days. As a result, companies collapsed, fortunes were lost overnight and confidence in the financial system disappeared. The effect of the Wall Street Crash would hit the United States first and hardest, and then plunge much of the world into a depression.

QUEUING FOR FOOD

In the US, factories and places of work closed, millions faced unemployment, eviction from their homes and terrible poverty. For those lucky enough to have work, wages plummeted, as did the demand for goods. Rural communities suffered from a drop in the prices of wheat, corn and meat, and farmers left grain to rot in the fields, along with slaughtered animals, as they couldn't afford to feed or transport them. In the towns and cities, long queues (known as 'bread lines') formed outside factories and soup kitchens by those in search of work and food.

Unemployed men line up outside a soup kitchen in Chicago, US.

1924

The US stock market starts to rise dramatically.

1929

March

Herbert Hoover becomes President of the US.

August

The USA enters a recession. Production declines and prices fall.

> ## "WHAT'S THE USE OF LOOKING FOR WORK ANY MORE; THERE ISN'T ANY. AND LOOK AT THE CHILDREN. HOW WOULD YOU FEEL IF YOU SAW YOUR OWN KIDS LIKE THAT: HALF NAKED AND SICK..."
>
> Martha Gelhorn, 'Report on Massachusetts', 25 November 1934.

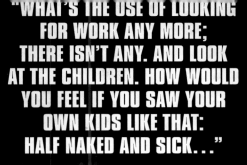

HOW CAN ANYTHING GOOD COME OUT OF A DEPRESSION?

With millions of people around the world having to cope with unemployment, homelessness and even starvation, can we really say that anything good came out of this period? We shall see that, despite all this suffering, some benefits did come out of this economic disaster and some things were improved. But with the economic downturns and depressions that have occurred since the Great Depression, can we really say that all of the lessons from this period have been learned?

HOOVERVILLES

Hundreds of shanty towns, known as 'Hoovervilles', cropped up around the USA during the Great Depression. They were named after President Hoover, who many people blamed for the Depression (see page 8). Hoovervilles were built by the homeless on empty land. Shacks were made out of boxes, bits of tin or any available material. One of the biggest Hoovervilles, standing in Seattle between 1931 and 1941, covered 3.5 hectares of land and housed 1,200 people.

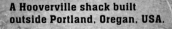

A Hooverville shack built outside Portland, Oregan, USA.

24 October
The US stock market falls dramatically.

25 October
Stock market rallies a little.

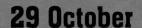

29 October
Stock market crashes. Known as Black Tuesday.

5

FINANCIAL PANIC

During the 1920s, known as the 'Roaring Twenties', the United States and much of the Western world enjoyed a period of economic prosperity. The USA had become the world's greatest industrial power and loans to Europe after World War I had made it the world's biggest trader and banker.

Crowds gather outside the New York Stock Exchange on Black Tuesday.

STOCK MARKET CRASH

The economic optimism of the 1920s led many people in the USA to invest their money in stocks, which are shares in the ownership of companies. The value of these stocks had risen, making investors money and encouraging more people to buy shares. This came to an abrupt end, however, in October 1929, when the prices of stocks fell. Panic selling by investors led to a further fall in prices, so that by 29 October (known as Black Tuesday) stock prices had collapsed completely, with shares worth only a fraction of their original value. The results were disastrous: banks lost huge amounts, businesses closed and the public stopped buying goods. The resulting economic depression would ripple across the USA and many parts of the world.

> "SPECULATORS MAY DO NO HARM AS BUBBLES ON A STEADY STREAM OF ENTERPRISE. BUT THE SITUATION IS SERIOUS WHEN ENTERPRISE BECOMES THE BUBBLE ON A WHIRLPOOL OF SPECULATION."
>
> British economist John Maynard Keynes, 1935.

1930

March
More than 3.2 million people are unemployed in the USA.

September–December
The first bank failures in the USA.

1931

February
Food riots occur in parts of the US.

May
Austria's leading bank (Creditanstalt) becomes insolvent.

Before the Crash, people used cheap loans to buy products such as this Ford Model T car.

CAUSES OF THE CRASH

Historians are divided as to what actually caused the Crash and the Great Depression. Key factors leading to the Crash included an increase in demand for goods. This had been funded by easy 'buy now pay later' loans. When the bad times came, households were unable to pay off their loans and many people lost their savings as a result. Also, the stock market had become overheated, with hugely confident investors speculating recklessly. This created an 'economic bubble' which burst dramatically on Black Tuesday.

Farmers in the USA had increased production in the 1920s although competition from Australia, Asia and Latin America had led to a surplus and fall in prices. The Crash caused prices to plummet even further.

★ GREAT DEPRESSION FIGURES ★

Name: John Maynard Keynes

Lived: 1883–1946

Job: Economist

In the 1930s, the British economist John Maynard Keynes developed the idea that governments could help to end 'boom and bust' economic cycles. Keynes believed that government spending, increasing the money supply and tax cuts could lessen the impact of a depression. President Roosevelt's New Deal programme was in line with Keynes's ideas.

With prices for crops falling, many people abandoned farms, like this one in Texas.

1932

July
There's a crisis in the German banking system.

21 September
Britain leaves the gold standard.

November
Franklin D Roosevelt is elected President of the USA.

DEPRESSION IN THE US

NAME: HERBERT HOOVER
LIVED: 1874–1964
JOB: US PRESIDENT

As the Depression worsened in the USA, the public increasingly blamed the Republican President Herbert Hoover for the problems they faced. He took office in 1929 and immediately took action when the Depression hit, urging the states to create jobs through public works. He refused, however, to direct relief payments to those in need and his efforts failed to revive the economy. As a result, Hoover lost the presidential elections of 1932, and voters elected the Democrat Franklin D Roosevelt by a big margin.

The effects of the Wall Street Crash were catastrophic in the USA. More than 5,000 banks closed between 1930 and 1933. Millions of Americans lost most of their savings and some parts of the country almost ran out of money, with many people resorting to bartering.

WORSENING TIMES

As the Depression deepened in 1931–1932, farmers and businesses went out of business and about 15 million people were unemployed at a time when there was no welfare for the jobless or their dependents. Those who had a job saw their wages drop by 50 per cent, consumers stopped buying goods and industrial output had, by 1932, halved.

As a result, a huge number of men, women and children sank into desperate poverty and hunger. The unemployed and destitute lost their homes, ending up in hastily built Hoovervilles (see page 5), while breadline queues outside factories and soup kitchens formed in every city. In 1931, more than 20,000 Americans committed suicide. And, according to one estimate, 34 million people out of its 123 million population had no income at all.

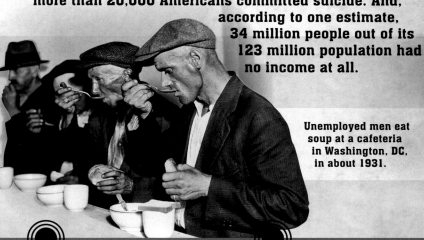

Unemployed men eat soup at a cafeteria in Washington, DC, in about 1931.

1933

January
Adolf Hitler comes to power in Germany.

April
The Civilian Conservation Corps (CCC) is established in the USA to work in national forests and parks.

May
The Tennessee Valley Authority is created with the aim of building dams, making fertiliser and developing federal land.

"THE WITHERED LEAVES OF INDUSTRIAL ENTERPRISE LIE ON EVERY SIDE; FARMERS FIND NO MARKETS FOR THEIR PRODUCE; THE SAVINGS OF MANY YEARS IN THOUSANDS OF FAMILIES ARE GONE. MORE IMPORTANT, A HOST OF UNEMPLOYED CITIZENS FACE THE GRIM PROBLEM OF EXISTENCE, AND AN EQUALLY GREAT NUMBER TOIL WITH LITTLE RETURN."

US President Franklin D Roosevelt in his inaugural address.

THE DUST BOWL

In the mid-west of the United States, severe drought in the early 1930s turned fields into 'Dust Bowls', with dust storms sweeping across the country to the east coast. Thousands of families were forced to leave the region. Only by the early 1940s, as a result of federal aid and better farming methods, did the area recover.

A farm in South Dakota lies almost submerged beneath a thick layer of dust, dropped by a severe dust storm in 1936.

1934

October

The Civil Works Administration is established to construct bridges, schools, hospitals and other government buildings.

May

A three-day dust storm blows a huge amount of soil off large areas of the west and south-west.

A dust storm approaches a farm in Texas.

DEPRESSION WORLDWIDE

The economic depression soon spread across the globe as US banks called in their loans around the world and the government raised taxes (known as tariffs) on imports and exports. As industry declined in the USA, the demand for raw materials fell, which affected Latin America, Asia and Africa in particular. World prices for commodities such as wheat, coffee and copper plunged, with global industrial production declining by as much as 37 per cent between 1929 and 1933.

DECLINING DEMAND

In South Africa, demand for agricultural and mineral exports fell dramatically, reducing many of its farmers to poverty. Because of high levels of US and British investment, the Depression severely damaged some Latin American countries, particularly Bolivia, Peru and Chile, with the export industry across Latin America badly affected.

Unemployed men in Canada march in protest about the lack of job opportunities.

CANADA
-42.4%

UNITED STATES
-46.8%

BRAZIL
-7.0%

ARGENTINA
-17.0%

1935

April
Roosevelt creates the Works Progress Administration, which will employ more than 8.5 million people.

August
The Social Security Act of 1935 is passed.

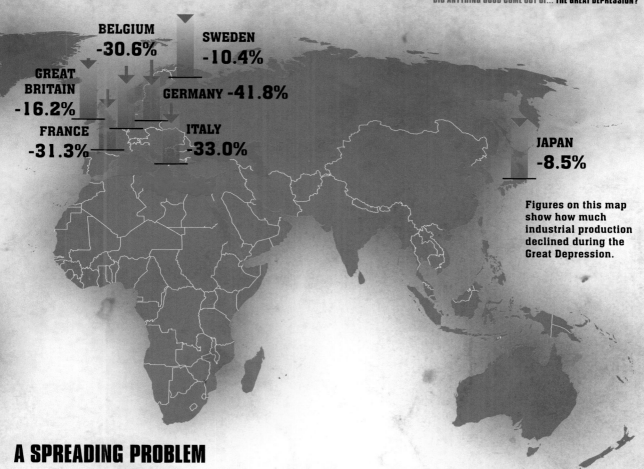

BELGIUM
-30.6%

SWEDEN
-10.4%

GREAT BRITAIN
-16.2%

GERMANY -41.8%

FRANCE
-31.3%

ITALY
-33.0%

JAPAN
-8.5%

Figures on this map show how much industrial production declined during the Great Depression.

A SPREADING PROBLEM

In Europe, the banking system in Central and Eastern Europe disintegrated. Germany, hugely reliant on American loans, suffered high unemployment, although its economy began to recover after its chancellor, Adolf Hitler, abandoned reparation payments (compensation paid to Allied nations after World War I) and began to pour money into the army and public works. Great Britain's industrial north suffered more severely than in the south, with unemployment reaching around 20 per cent. France, which was more self-sufficient in food, suffered less than other industrial countries. Only the Soviet Union was entirely unaffected by the Great Depression. Under the communist dictatorship of Joseph Stalin, the Soviet Union was undergoing a period of industrialisation and was isolated from the world economy.

1938

European countries start to emerge from recession as they prepare for war.

1939

The USA emerges from recession as it starts to build up its armed forces. From 1939 to 1941, US manufacturing rises by 50 per cent.

AFTERMATH

Protesters gather outside the offices of a US bank after its collapse.

As the Depression took hold across the world, many countries tried to protect their economies by restricting foreign trade, limiting imports from other nations and placing tariffs on them (a policy known as 'protectionism'). In many countries, government regulation of the economy, especially of financial markets, increased substantially in the 1930s.

RECOVERY AROUND THE WORLD

Recovery from the Depression varied greatly throughout the world. In the USA, the new president Franklin D Roosevelt introduced an economic programme known as the New Deal. In 1933, the USA saw some recovery although it suffered another severe downturn in 1937–1938, and the Depression would only completely come to an end after the outbreak of war in 1939.

Britain saw glimmers of recovery as early as 1931 after it abandoned the gold standard (the system by which a country's currency was defined in terms of gold – see page 23). Germany and Japan similarly began to recover in 1932–1933, as did Canada, Australia and some European countries. France experienced the Depression a little later than other nations, and began to recover in 1938.

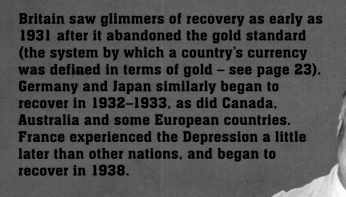

President Roosevelt signs the Social Security Act in 1935, which guaranteed income for the unemployed and those who had retired.

THE RISE OF EXTREMISM

In other countries, the economic slump created conditions that favoured the rise of fascism and totalitarian states (one-party states where the government seeks to control all aspects of life). These included Adolf Hitler's Nazi Party in Germany.

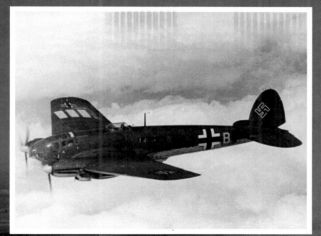

The push to rearm in the run-up to World War II and build weapons of war, such as this German Heinkel bomber (left) and this fighter factory in the USA(main image), actually improved economic conditions in many countries.

GREAT DEPRESSION FIGURES

NAME: **FRANKLIN DELANO ROOSEVELT**

LIVED: **1882–1945**

JOB: **US PRESIDENT**

Confined to a wheelchair after contracting polio in 1921, Roosevelt won a resounding victory in the 1932 elections. With the USA still in the grip of economic depression, Roosevelt introduced a New Deal package of economic measures in 1933 designed to lift the USA and its people out of economic crisis. During World War II, he played an important part in the Allied war effort and became the first US president to secure a fourth term of presidency just before his death in 1945.

RISE OF FASCISM

In the 1920s, Germany was already crippled by high reparation payments and high inflation. The withdrawal of US loans after 1929 had a bad effect on Germany, with unemployment rising to 6 million. Banks closed, families lost their life savings and many were unable to buy essential items with money that was virtually worthless.

THE TREATY OF VERSAILLES

The Treaty of Versailles which ended World War I demanded that Germany surrender large areas of land to the Allies, limit its army to 100,000 men and pay huge fines, or reparations. Many people thought that the treaty was too harsh and the payments excessive. Some historians have also argued that the Great Depression and the rise of totalitarian states were a result of the harsh terms of the Treaty of Versailles.

> **"THE TREATY INCLUDES NO PROVISIONS FOR THE ECONOMIC REHABILITATION OF EUROPE – NOTHING TO MAKE THE DEFEATED CENTRAL EMPIRES INTO GOOD NEIGHBOURS, NOTHING TO STABILISE THE NEW STATES OF EUROPE."**
>
> John Maynard Keynes writing in *The Economic Consequences of the Peace*, 1919.

Four of the leaders of the victorious Allied powers standing outside the Palace of Versailles. From left to right: British prime minister, David Lloyd George, Italian prime minister, Vittorio Emanuele Orlando, French prime minister, Georges Clemenceau and US president, Woodrow Wilson.

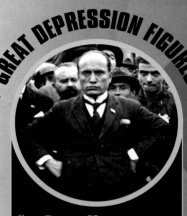

GREAT DEPRESSION FIGURES

NAME: BENITO MUSSOLINI
LIVED: 1883–1945
JOB: ITALIAN FASCIST LEADER

The ideology of fascism was developed by Benito Mussolini, who gained power in Italy in 1922. Fascism was a totalitarian system that attempted to impose a military discipline on society at the expense of individual freedom. The economic slump in Italy coincided with a more aggressive foreign policy, with Mussolini conquering Ethiopia in 1935.

POLITICAL EXTREMES

From this social and economic chaos rose the National Socialist German Workers' Party, or Nazi Party. Its leader Adolf Hitler grew in popularity by promising to create jobs, expand German territory and restore German pride by rejecting the punishing terms of the Treaty of Versailles. He blamed the economic crisis on Jewish financiers and communists and he appealed to those left angry by years of hardship. Many people thought the Nazis could provide a 'strong' government. In the economic turmoil, some German workers had also turned to communism, which led frightened businessmen and industrialists to finance Hitler's campaign.

Hitler's book *Mein Kampf* ('My Struggle') set out his political beliefs and his plans for the future of Germany.

By the time the Nazis took power in 1933, Nazi Party membership had grown to 2 million. Appointing himself leader in 1934, Hitler assumed total control of the country, drastically reducing unemployment by pouring money into public work schemes, building up his armed forces and opening factories to build military equipment.

GERMAN HYPERINFLATION

Prices soared in Germany during the early 1920s.

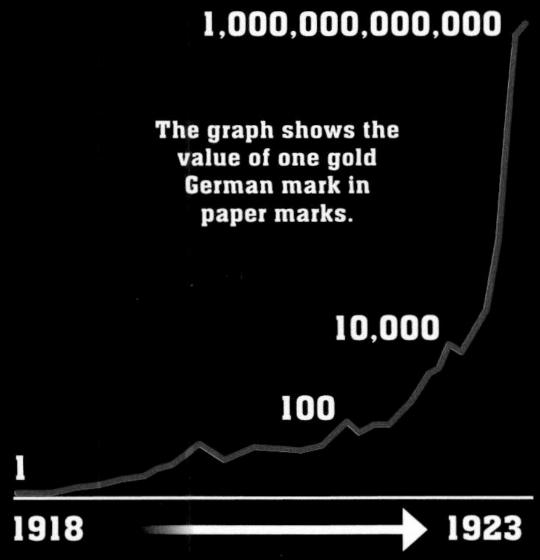

1,000,000,000,000

The graph shows the value of one gold German mark in paper marks.

10,000

100

1

1918   →   1923

Hitler salutes a parade of Nazi SA troops in Nuremberg in 1935 following his rise to power.

A MOVE TO THE RIGHT

Elsewhere in the world other totalitarian movements emerged. Political division in Spain led to three years of civil war from 1936 and the establishment of a nationalist regime. This lasted until the death of its leader, General Francisco Franco, in 1975. In 1933, Austrian Chancellor Dollfuss established a one-party dictatorship largely based on Italian fascism, after arguments broke out between other political parties.

Explosions rock the city of Barcelona during the Spanish Civil War.

Spanish anti-fascists raise a banner above a street which reads 'They shall not pass!'

FASCISM IN EUROPE

In many parts of Europe, fascist movements grew in strength: the fascist Iron Guard soared in popularity in Romania after 1933, and a variety of governments that borrowed elements from fascism came to power in Greece, Yugoslavia, Poland and Lithuania. In 1934, France saw mass rioting by the fascist Francist and far-right movements, and in Britain Oswald Mosley formed the British Union of Fascists in 1932, which claimed 50,000 members.

Getúlio Vargas remained in power in Brazil until 1945.

SOUTH AMERICA

Brazil was badly affected by the slump in coffee prices and the effects of the Great Depression. Social unrest led to revolution in 1930, with the leader Getúlio Vargas forming a one-party dictatorship by 1938. In the 1930s, the fascist National Socialist Movement of Chile gained seats in the government, which led to a massacre in 1938 when they attempted to seize power.

THE FAR EAST

Japan, unable to trade with the United States, searched elsewhere for raw materials and markets. Military leaders, many of whom thought that Japan's economic problems could only be solved by force, invaded the Chinese province of Manchuria in 1931 (right). By 1937, Japan and China were at war. Japan had also made agreements with fascist Italy and Germany, and it invaded French and British colonies in Southeast Asia when it entered World War II.

RUSSIA

Manchuria

CHINA

Beijing

KOREA

JAPAN

By 1931, Japanese troops (below) had seized Korea and large areas of Manchuria in China.

A BETTER DEAL?

President Roosevelt had promised Americans that he would tackle the Great Depression with a 'New Deal'. This programme would deal with the three 'R's of: 'Relief' of poverty by feeding the starving and reducing unemployment; 'Recovery' to get everyone working again; and 'Reform' of the financial system to prevent the Depression happening again.

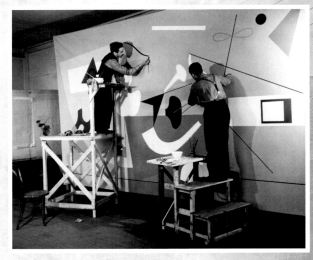

The 1939 New York World's Fair was a public scheme aimed at boosting the economy. Artist Ilya Bolotowsky (above, left) painted a giant mural for the event.

FIRESIDE CHATS

Roosevelt's reforms inspired confidence and trust both in the US people and in the financial markets. In his first hundred days, he shut all the banks, checked their accounts and decided which ones could open again, creating confidence in the banking system so that money flowed in again. He also formed various agencies, which pumped money into public work schemes, such as bridges and roads, and the building of 33 dams in the Tennessee Valley. He provided money for emergency relief, for clothing, schools and employment schemes, and lent money to farmers and home-owners.

Between 1933 and 1944, Roosevelt made a series of radio broadcasts, known as 'fireside chats'. In these he talked directly to the American people and tried to calm fears about the Depression.

★ GREAT DEPRESSION FIGURES ★

NAME: ELEANOR ROOSEVELT
LIVED: 1884–1962
JOB: US FIRST LADY

Eleanor Roosevelt was the longest-serving first lady in US history. During her husband's time as president, she campaigned strongly for human rights, and led an active professional life as a speaker and writer. She also played a key role in establishing a model town for unemployed miners and their families in 1933, although many considered this project a failure.

The construction of huge hydroelectric dams, such as this one being built in Oregon in 1934, was a key part of the New Deal project.

★ ENEMY OF FASCISM ★

DID IT WORK?

Historians are divided over the success of the New Deal. Some think that it may have actually prolonged the Depression. The economy only temporarily improved before it took another sharp downturn in 1937, and the decline lingered until the United States entered World War II in 1941. They argue the New Deal cost billions of dollars but failed to solve the problem. Others argue that the New Deal was a success; that it provided relief and jobs for those who needed it and helped to revive business.

The crisis of the Great Depression and the rise of Nazi Germany led also to a renewed interest in Soviet communism among US intellectuals. In its various alliances, the Soviet Union (national flag, left) appeared to be the uncompromising opponent to fascism. It also had an apparently successful economy in contrast to the near-collapse of capitalism elsewhere.

TURNING INWARDS

While some countries moved to political extremism during the Depression, other democratic nations around the world turned inwards and tried to protect their own economies by taxing imports (which ultimately damaged world trade) and focusing on their own finances, unemployment and economic hardship.

Ramsey MacDonald led the British governments in the 1930s.

PROTECT THE EMPIRE

In Britain, disputes within the Labour government led to the formation in 1931 of an emergency National Government, dominated by the Conservatives. Forced to abandon the gold standard (see page 23) in 1931, which helped recovery, the government abandoned free trade in favour of protecting its colonies. This involved introducing a tariff on all imports, except those from the British Empire. In August 1931, the government replaced an unemployment scheme with one based on need rather than the level of contributions.

British Prime Minister Neville Chamberlain, seen here with the Italian dictator, Benito Mussolini, was accused of appeasing Europe's fascist regimes.

LUCE

The Sydney Harbour Bridge was opened in 1932 at the height of the Great Depression.

DELAYING REARMAMENT

At the same time, Britain delayed rearmament (building up its weapons) until 1936 and minimised its commitments in Europe. To save money, France also delayed rearmament, cut its defence spending and, in alliance with Britain, pursued a policy of appeasement (making concessions in order to avoid war) even in the face of Nazi aggression. When war finally broke out, many thought appeasement had allowed Hitler to grow strong.

In the lead-up to World War II, many British weapons, such as this biplane fighter, were old and out-dated.

AUSTRALIA AND NEW ZEALAND

As New Zealand relied almost totally on exporting its farm produce, it was badly hit by the Depression, and suffered very high unemployment levels. The government in power tried to implement spending cuts, but seemed unable to deal with the problems, leading to the first-time victory of the Labour government in 1935. They immediately set about helping the needy; farmers were guaranteed prices for their produce and a number of reforms reorganised the social welfare system. Like New Zealand, Australia, too, suffered badly from the Depression, and its important export industry was severely hit. However, increases in the price of gold and of wool after 1933 enabled the country to recover quickly.

21

FINANCIAL REGULATION

The Great Depression changed the world economy in many ways. In order to prevent another banking crisis, several governments in the 1930s increased regulation of the economy, especially of financial markets. In the USA, the government established a special commission in 1934 to oversee stock market trading practices.

BANKING PROTECTION

In 1933, the Banking Act established deposit insurance, a measure that protected people's savings should the banks run into financial problems. This helped to avoid bank runs (everyone withdrawing money from the banks), which contributed to the general panic of the Great Depression. Deposit insurance is now implemented in many countries around the world.

The Mount Washington Hotel in New Hampshire, USA, where the 1944 Bretton Woods Conference was held.

FINANCIAL COOPERATION

In 1944, an international conference, known as the Bretton Woods Conference, looked at ways to rebuild nations after World War II and create economic cooperation between countries. Key to its aim was that international trade should be encouraged. This led to the formation of the World Bank, which provides loans to poor countries and aims to eliminate world poverty, and the International Monetary Fund (IMF), which promotes international cooperation. Also created after World War II was GATT, the forerunner of the World Trade Organisation.

A meeting of the World Trade Organisation, which regulates free trade.

★ GOLD STANDARD ★

Before World War I, the currencies of many countries were based on gold and could be exchanged for gold at fixed rates. During the 1920s, many countries returned to the gold standard (including Britain, France and the USA) but the Great Depression forced countries off it again. Many historians blame the gold standard for prolonging the Great Depression and allowing it to spread, as the US government couldn't create money to stimulate the economy and fund failing banks. At the Bretton Woods Conference, a new international monetary system was established. This was based on fixed exchange rates like the gold standard, but differed in that countries could borrow from the IMF instead of relying on their gold reserves.

WORKERS' RIGHTS

Trade unions, formed by workers who join together to protect their wages and working rights, saw a great surge in membership in the USA during the Great Depression. In 1933, there were 2.7 million trade unions members, most belonging to skilled craft unions. By 1939, this number had tripled.

Workers from the American Teamsters union fight with police in Minneapolis during a strike in 1934.

ANTI-UNION

In the early 1930s, the much larger numbers of workers in the mass production industries, such as textiles, automobiles and steel, were poorly represented. Employers were often strongly opposed to unions, firing employees if they were sympathetic to a union or halting strikes by court action.

Left: American workers line up to join a union in the late 1930s.

Below: Banner of the Electrical, Radio and Machine Workers Union from 1940.

"IN THE HEART OF THE GREAT DEPRESSION, MILLIONS OF AMERICAN WORKERS DID SOMETHING THEY'D NEVER DONE BEFORE: THEY JOINED A UNION. EMBOLDENED BY THE PASSAGE OF THE WAGNER ACT, WHICH MADE COLLECTIVE BARGAINING EASIER, UNIONS ORGANISED INDUSTRIES ACROSS THE COUNTRY, REMAKING THE ECONOMY."

James Surowiecki in *State of the Unions*, *The New Yorker*, 17 January 2011.

TOGETHER WE STAND

New Deal legislation passed in 1933 and 1935 led to great changes for workers' rights. It helped to increase wages and prices, and enabled workers to negotiate better wages and working conditions with employers (known as collective bargaining). Businesses were required to act fairly with trade union members, and not simply fire them. Unskilled workers were also organised into unions with the help of the Congress of Industrial Organizations. Steel, auto, rubber and other mass production workers formed unions so that by the end of the 1930s union membership had grown from 2.7 million in 1933 to 8.5 million.

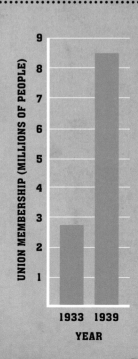

UNION MEMBERSHIP (MILLIONS OF PEOPLE)

1933   1939

YEAR

A SAFETY NET

By the early 1930s, the USA lagged far behind many countries in Europe in support for the unemployed and those in need. The people of America, unlike many other industrial nations, were forced to cope with the effects of the Depression without any national system of social security.

HELPING THE NEEDY

New Deal legislation, in particular the Social Security Act of 1935, marked a radical change in US social policy. It helped to provide unemployment insurance, a state pension and it supported handicapped people and mothers with young children. This new legislation was not without its opponents, though, with many in the USA believing that social security went against the US principle of self-help.

Dorothea Lange's photograph of a migrant mother and her children captures the stress and suffering of people during the Great Depression.

GREAT DEPRESSION FIGURES

Name: **DOROTHEA LANGE**

Lived: **1895–1965**

Job: **PHOTOGRAPHER**

One of the leading photographers of her day, Dorothea Lange is perhaps best known for her images of migrant workers and sharecroppers during the Great Depression.

"FRANKLIN ROOSEVELT'S NEW DEAL PROMISED SECURITY AND SUCCOUR TO THOSE IN NEED."

John F Kennedy, 'The New Frontier Speech', 1960.

CRADLE TO GRAVE

In Britain, earlier legislation had put in place compulsory national unemployment and health insurance schemes, although this was paid out according to contributions rather than need. During the Depression, many people had been too poor to make contributions and were left destitute as a result. In 1931, a new unemployment benefit system was introduced, based on need rather than contribution. After World War II, the Labour government used this as the foundation for their 'cradle-to-grave' welfare state system, which would provide a comprehensive system of social insurance, and the new National Health Service.

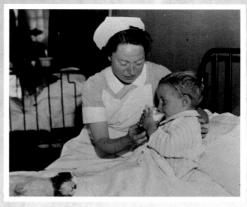

Britain's National Health Service, founded in 1948, offered free health care for all.

LATIN AMERICA

In Latin America, governments improved welfare institutions that helped millions of workers to achieve a better standard of living. Brazilian President Vargas did much to improve conditions for the poor. He established an eight-hour work day, abolished child labour and provided medical care for pregnant mothers and sick workers. In Colombia in 1934, newly elected president Alfonso López Pumarejo introduced the eight-hour work day and the right of workers to strike. In 1934, Mexican president General Lázaro Cárdenas, who served from 1934 to 1940, aimed to improve the lives of the Mexican people with a six-year plan to advance agriculture and industry.

A painting shows President Cárdenas, watched by Mexican peasants, signing a land reform bill that redistributed millions of acres of land from landowners to peasants.

EFFECTS ON WOMEN AND MINORITIES

Extreme poverty in the USA led to a decline in the birth rate, postponement of marriage (largely due to the expense) and a drop in divorces, as it was cheaper for men just to abandon their wives than pay for divorce.

WOMEN AT WAR

Although women were not included in any of the New Deal labour initiatives, their employment rose during the 1930s, largely because they were cheaper to hire than men. The Social Security Act, with its support for families with dependent children and for mothers, benefited women to some extent. However, its provisions for pensions excluded domestic servants and farm labourers, two groups that were largely female and black.

For African Americans, the Depression worsened their already poor circumstances. They were often the first people to be fired from jobs, and in early assistance programmes black people often received far less than white people and were sometimes excluded from soup kitchens. The New Deal welfare policies were of benefit to some black Americans – low-cost public housing was made available to them and other programmes provided jobs, the opportunity to form trade unions and enabled some black youths to continue with their education.

> "WE DO NOT CONSIDER IT CORRECT FOR THE WOMAN TO INTERFERE IN THE WORLD OF MAN."
>
> Adolf Hitler, speech to the NSDAP Women's Organisation, September 1934.

Black unemployed women gather in a camp arranged by the Federal Emergency Relief of Administration in 1936.

★ NEW ZEALAND ★

In New Zealand, the new Labour party, which first won power in 1935, set up a welfare state as a result of the Depression and introduced a series of reforms to better the lives of the Maori people, from the provision of education for children to improving housing and access to medical care.

The Nazis tried to boost the birth rate by improving maternity care and rewarding mothers for having large families.

NAZI GERMANY

In Germany, the Nazis' view that women should stay at home rather than go out to work was reinforced by unemployment in the 1920s. Hitler claimed that the 'emancipation of women' was a slogan invented by Jewish intellectuals.

When Hitler came to power, he took action to reduce the number of women working as he believed women were unable to 'think logically or reason objectively, since they are ruled only by emotion'. The Nazis' racist assertion of the superiority of the Aryan 'master race' and its blaming of the Depression on the Jewish population ultimately led to the persecution and eventual mass murder of 6 million Jews, along with other ethnic 'undesirables'. These included Poles, Russians, Gypsies, black and mixed-race people and the mentally and physically handicapped.

PUBLIC WORKS

To counteract the effects of the Depression, some governments, particularly in the USA, poured money into public work schemes in order to generate employment. This left some of the longest-lasting legacies of the Great Depression.

PUTTING PEOPLE TO WORK

One New Deal initiative, the Works Progress Administration, put 8.5 million people to work building 15,000 public buildings, 75,000 bridges, 800 airports and 1 million km of roads, along with canals, universities and sewage systems. Most of the spending and work came in two waves, 1933–1935 and 1938, creating infrastructure and public services that are still in use today across the USA. Some of public works projects include the Lincoln Tunnel in New York State and the Overseas Highway connecting Key West in Florida to the mainland.

The Bahia Honda Rail Bridge in the Florida Keys was converted for highway use with federal funds in 1938. It remained in use until 1972,

"IF YOU PUT A LIGHT ON EVERY FARM, YOU PUT A LIGHT IN EVERY HEART."

Motto of The Rural Electrification Administration (REA).

The Lincoln Tunnel runs beneath the Hudson River, linking Manhattan and New Jersey. Construction began in 1934.

HOOVER DAM AND LAS VEGAS

New Deal programmes also transformed the generation and distribution of electrical supply in the US. Low-interest loans funded the running of cables carrying electricity to rural areas so that by 1939 a quarter of farms had electricity compared to one in ten in 1932. The Boulder Dam, later renamed the Hoover Dam after President Herbert Hoover, was constructed on the Colorado River in Nevada between 1931 and 1936. A massive undertaking, thousands of workers were involved in its construction. Las Vegas, then a small mining town, housed the many thousands of workers – the arrival of whom helped the town avoid the worst of the Depression, and enabled it to grow into the 'The Entertainment Capital of the World'.

When it was completed, the Hoover Dam (above and below) was the largest structure ever built in concrete.

BUILDING AND INDUSTRY BOOM

In Britain, the Great Depression hit industry located in northern England, south Wales and central Scotland particularly hard, especially older industries such as coal mining and steel manufacturing.

HOUSING BOOST

South and central England, where newer, less export-reliant industries were based, were less affected. In fact, from 1932, the south experienced a housing boom, with more houses built than any other year since. Many of the suburban districts that are still very much visible across southern England (main image), were built in the 1930s.

The boost in house building was made possible by the government's reduction in interest rates (the percentage of money paid for a loan) and more affordable mortgages (a loan to buy a house) so that normal working people could enter the housing market. The cost of constructing houses was also relatively cheap, an added incentive for house-builders.

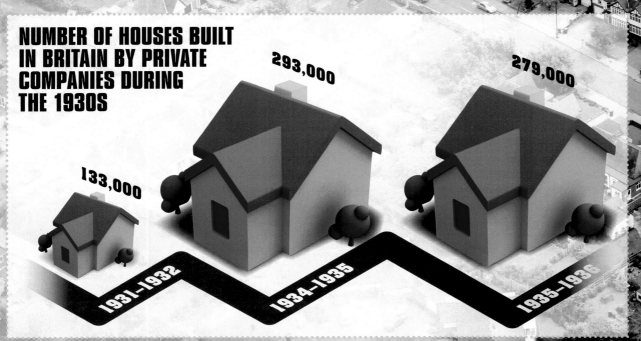

NUMBER OF HOUSES BUILT IN BRITAIN BY PRIVATE COMPANIES DURING THE 1930S

133,000 — 1931-1932

293,000 — 1934-1935

279,000 — 1935-1936

THE MOTOR INDUSTRY

The 1930s in Britain also saw significant growth in the production of cars. From 1919 to 1938, the number of cars on the road grew from around 100,000 to 2 million. Morris and Austin remained the two leading producers, although Ford enjoyed considerable success, particularly when it launched its first £100 four-seater car in 1935. The more affordable price of cars led to wider ownership. With more cars on the road, new safety measures were introduced in the 1930s. These included compulsory driving tests, set speed limits in built-up areas, safety glass in cars and the first 'cat's eyes' on the road.

Cat's eyes reflect a car's headlights, and show the middle and edges of the road.

The Austin 7 was one of Britain's most popular cars in the 1930s.

CREATIVE THINKING

Despite the difficulties of the Great Depression, many advances were made in technology and science during the 1930s. Difficult times can sometimes force people to think more creatively, improving products and creating demand for them even when money is tight. Unemployment or economic hardship can also force some talented people to come up with new ideas and innovations.

★ PHOTOCOPIERS

In 1933 Chester Carlson, like millions of others in the US, was laid off from his job at the Bell Telephone Laboratories. Unemployed, he earned a law degree and took a job in the patent department of a New York electronics firm. Frustrated with having to hand-copy patent drawings, he experimented with dry photocopying techniques, using electrostatic attraction to stick powder to plain paper. Making his first breakthrough in 1938, he received a patent in 1942 and in 1959 Xerox sold the first automatic photocopier.

A replica of Chester Carlson's original Xerox copier, which was first made in 1948.

★ VW BEETLE

As part of his drive to reverse the economic decline in Germany, Adolf Hitler wanted a cheap, simple car that could be mass produced. In late 1934, Porsche was given a state contract to develop the Volkswagen ('people's car'). In 1937, Daimler Benz took over production and in 1938 a factory was built dedicated to production. The Beetle (below), as it came to be known, went on to become one of the most popular car designs ever, with over 21 million models sold.

"IT WAS KIND OF A HARD STRUGGLE. SO I THOUGHT THE POSSIBILITY OF MAKING AN INVENTION MIGHT KILL TWO BIRDS WITH ONE STONE; IT WOULD BE A CHANCE TO DO THE WORLD SOME GOOD AND ALSO A CHANCE TO DO MYSELF SOME GOOD."

Chester Carlson, inventor of the photocopier.

★ INDUSTRIAL DESIGN

US illustrator Raymond Loewy was convinced that better product design was part of the solution to the Depression, helping to increase sales and cut costs. In 1929, Sigmund Gestetner, a British manufacturer of office duplicating machines, commissioned Loewy to redesign his clunky-looking machine. Loewy designed a sleeker and safer version. He also designed a streamlined locomotive, replacing riveting with welding, saving millions of dollars in manufacture. Industrial design is now a key component in manufacturing.

The streamlined PRR S1 locomotive was designed by Raymond Loewy.

★ MONOPOLY

Monopoly is now available in 111 countries and is one of the world's best-selling board games.

US salesman Charles Darrow lost his job after the Wall Street Crash in 1929. He saw his friends and neighbours playing a board game which involved buying and selling property. The game was in fact a variation of 'The Landlord's Game', which was originally invented in 1904 by Elizabeth Magie. Darrow redesigned and sold the game, with the inclusion of some of the items found in the game today, like the Chance and Community Chest cards and the question mark on the Chance spaces. Parker Brothers eventually bought the rights to Darrow's game in 1935 and promoted it as the brainchild of an out-of work engineer seeking an affordable means of entertainment during the Depression.

★ OTHER INNOVATIONS

Other innovations that hit the market during the 1930s included the electric dry razor, the car radio and neoprene, which is a synthetic rubber. A research scientist, Wallace Carothers, working at the US company DuPont, recorded the initial discovery in 1931. It came on to the market in 1937 and it is now used in a huge range of products.

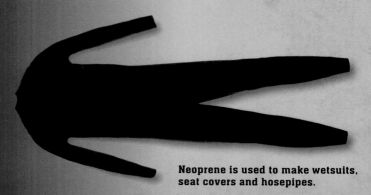

Neoprene is used to make wetsuits, seat covers and hosepipes.

35

CULTURE IN THE DEPRESSION

The Marx Brothers made some of the most popular comedy films of the period.

The social and economic turmoil in Germany and the spread of Nazism across Europe led to a large number of Europe's intellectuals and artists emigrating to the USA (via France and Britain) in the 1930s.

★ THE MOVIES

In cinema, the Great Depression also coincided with the introduction of the 'talkies' and by 1930 the silent film was practically extinct. For many people trying to scratch a living during the Depression, the cinema provided a cheap form of escapism. The most memorable movies of the 1930s were swashbuckling adventures, musicals and comedies. Few dealt with the plight of the poor. Audiences wanted to see the glamorous stars of Hollywood, such as Cary Grant, Mae West and Bette Davis. The Marx Brothers also rose to fame in the 1930s as did the child-star Shirley Temple.

★ A NEW HOME

Playwrights and novelists, such as Thomas Mann and Bertolt Brecht; musicians and composers, such as Igor Stravinsky, and painters and sculptors, notably Marc Chagall and Piet Mondrian, all made their homes in the US. By the end of the 1930s New York and Hollywood had largely replaced Vienna and Berlin as the home of Western culture.

Born in Russia in 1882, Igor Stravinsky later to moved to France before settling in the USA.

★ ESCAPING THE NAZIS

Fritz Lang (1890–1976), the Austrian-born screenplay writer and director, had a successful film career in the 1920s and early 1930s. When invited by Joseph Goebbels, the Nazi propaganda chief, to supervise German films, Lang immediately left for France and later moved to the USA. He enjoyed a flourishing career in Hollywood, and continued to direct films right through to the mid-1950s.

★ CHILD STAR

Between 1935 and 1938, Hollywood's number one box-office star was Shirley Temple (1928–2014). She found international fame at the age of six featuring in *Bright Eyes* (1934), in which she sang her signature song 'On the Good Ship Lollipop'. Her portrayal as a sweet, lovable child able to open her heart and charm stern old men created a feeling of hope and optimism during the gloom of the Depression era.

"IT IS A SPLENDID THING THAT FOR JUST 15 CENTS AN AMERICAN CAN GO TO A MOVIE AND LOOK AT THE SMILING FACE OF A BABY AND FORGET HIS TROUBLES."

US President Franklin D Roosevelt

At the height of her fame Shirley Temple was the highest-paid actor in the USA. Here she is sitting next to First Lady Eleanor Roosevelt.

FEDERAL ARTS

As part of the drive to create jobs in the USA, President Roosevelt's New Deal administration also created arts, writing and theatre projects. Writers were hired to record interviews with workers, fishermen, waitresses and ex-slaves for guidebooks covering the life and history of every state.

"A FEW GENERATIONS AGO, THE PEOPLE OF THIS COUNTRY WERE TAUGHT BY THEIR WRITERS AND THEIR CRITICS AND THEIR TEACHERS TO BELIEVE THAT ART WAS SOMETHING FOREIGN TO AMERICA AND TO THEMSELVES."

President Roosevelt talking about the Federal Art Project in 1941.

Painted by Julius Woeltz in 1942, this mural was funded by the Federal Art Project and can be found in a post office in Benton, Arkansas.

★ THE FEDERAL ART PROJECT

The largest of the New Deal arts programmes, the Federal Art Project found work for nearly 10,000 artists during the Great Depression. The artists were commissioned to produce murals in public buildings, as well as sculptures, posters, photography, theatre scenes, and arts and crafts. The project lasted from 1935 until 1943 and was responsible for the creation of about 200,000 works of art, some of which are still on display today. It supported artists such as Jackson Pollock and Willem de Kooning before they could earn money from their own art.

Muralist Eric Mose works on a public building fresco as part of the Federal Art Project in 1936.

A 1936 poster promoting a forum about the role of art and its future

★ THE FEDERAL MUSIC PROJECT

The Federal Music Project organised concerts, music classes, festivals and created new orchestras. In doing so, it provided work for musicians, conductors and composers during the Great Depression. It also commissioned studies into music from around the country, including cowboy music, Creole and the music of black slaves.

A Federal Music Project poster advertises a concert in New York in 1936.

★ THE FEDERAL THEATRE PROJECT

Providing work for actors, performers, writers and directors, the Federal Theatre Project organised plays, dance dramas, acting classes and even circus performances. It also organised a Living Newspapers project, where people cut out stories from newspapers and magazines and produced plays based on them.

RECORDING THE ERA

Writers, film makers and photographers were inspired by the great upheavals of the first half of the 20th century. These upheavals included two world wars and the economic depression of the 1930s, as well as more regional events, such as the Mexican Revolution of 1911.

LATIN AMERICA

Latin American writers started to look beyond their own countries, while other writers and poets dealt with themes such as the plight of indigenous people and social injustice. One of the most well-known South American novels of the period was *Doña Barbara* (1929) by Venezuelan writer Romulo Gallegos. It tells of Venezuela's struggles against injustice and US domination.

NAME: JOHN STEINBECK
LIVED: 1902–1968
JOB: WRITER

As well as *The Grapes of Wrath*, Steinbeck wrote other literary masterpieces including *Of Mice and Men* (1937) and *East of Eden* (1952). However, it is his story of a struggling family in the Depression for which he is most famous, and *The Grapes of Wrath* has sold more than 14 million copies around the world.

WRITERS IN THE US

In the USA, authors wrote about the breakdown of the economy and the gritty reality of the Depression. James T Farrell's trilogy *Studs Lonigan* (1932, 1935, 1936) depicted Irish Catholics, while Richard Wright's *Native Son* (1940) gave a stark portrait of a young African American living in poverty in Chicago. An immediate bestseller, it was the first protest novel that successfully attempted to explain the racial divide within society.

Richard Wright, author of *Native Son*.

THE GRAPES OF WRATH

John Steinbeck's novel *The Grapes of Wrath* (1939) captured the turbulence of the Depression in its depiction of farm workers living in the 'dust bowl' of the USA. Driven from their home in Oklahoma by drought and poverty, they take to the road in a battered old truck in search of work. The book was noted for its passionate depiction of the plight of the poor and became the best-selling book of 1939.

> "HOUSES WERE SHUT TIGHT, AND CLOTH WEDGED AROUND DOORS AND WINDOWS, BUT THE DUST CAME IN SO THINLY THAT IT COULD NOT BE SEEN IN THE AIR, AND IT SETTLED LIKE POLLEN ON THE CHAIRS AND TABLES, ON THE DISHES."

John Steinbeck, *The Grapes of Wrath*.

Actors and crew film a scene from the 1940 film of *The Grapes of Wrath*, directed by John Ford and starring Henry Fonda.

RECORDING LIFE

A documentary-style realism also influenced writers in the 1930s as they joined journalists and photographers to provide travelogue accounts and eye-witness portraits of shantytowns, tenant farmers and the very poor. Images such as Dorothea Lange's famous photos of migrant workers featured in *Life* magazine and helped to portray the harsh realities of life during the Depression.

An image from Dorothea Lange's famous series on migrant workers in the Depression.

41

SO DID ANYTHING GOOD COME OUT OF THE GREAT DEPRESSION?

LOSING HOPE

The Great Depression was an economic catastrophe, the effects of which would be felt across the world. In the USA, millions of citizens found themselves without work or homes, with men, women and children forced to live in poverty and hunger.

Unemployed British workers gather outside a closed factory in the early 1930s.

> "AND THE LITTLE SCREAMING FACT THAT SOUNDS THROUGH ALL HISTORY: REPRESSION WORKS ONLY TO STRENGTHEN AND KNIT THE REPRESSED."
>
> John Steinbeck, *The Grapes of Wrath*.

ECONOMIC SLUMP

The economic crisis caused turmoil across the world, leading to the disintegration of the banking system in parts of Europe and 6 million people unemployed in Germany. As industry declined, the demand for raw materials slumped, affecting nations right across Africa, Asia and South America.

In the USA, which suffered the worst during the Depression, starvation was a real threat for people and many found themselves in the countless bread lines outside soup kitchens and the Hooverville slums that appeared across the nation. Those who suffered began to lose hope in the American dream, a feeling reflected in much of the literature of the time.

EXTREMISM AND WAR

Elsewhere, the economic and social chaos created the perfect environment for the overthrow of democracy and the emergence of brutal regimes. In Germany, rising unemployment and economic hardship increased support for Adolf Hitler and the Nazi Party, and his assumption of power in Germany. The social and economic turmoil of the Great Depression would ultimately lead to World War II.

Hitler's drive for German expansion had its origins in the humiliation of World War I and the struggles of the Great Depression.

"DREADFUL APATHY, UNSURENESS AND DISCOURAGEMENT SEEM TO HAVE FALLEN UPON OUR LIFE."

Critic Edmund Wilson in 1931.

A ground crew member directs a US P-51 Mustang fighter towards take-off during World War II. The conflict remains the deadliest in human history.

POSITIVE EFFECTS OF THE GREAT DEPRESSION

In many parts of the world, the Depression led to the introduction of far-reaching economic and social reforms, designed to tackle unemployment and poverty and prevent another financial crisis.

Offices of the World Bank in Washington, DC.

★ INTERNATIONAL COOPERATION

As a result of the Depression and World War II, greater cooperation now exists between the nations of the world with the establishment of the World Bank, IMF and World Trade Organization. These agencies aim to regulate world trade, provide loans to developing countries and get rid of world poverty. While fascist and totalitarian regimes emerged during the years of the Depression, some would argue that these grew in response to the destruction of World War I and the peace terms that followed it.

★ GREATER FREEDOM

In many parts of Latin America, the USA and Britain had invested heavily in industry, particularly in oil production. This had led to a growing US/British influence in Latin America, with US oil companies in Mexico even able to restrict land reform programmes and threaten military intervention. During the years of the Depression, countries like Mexico and Peru were able to break free of this domination and develop new local industry, including oil exploration (left) and welfare provision for their workers.

"FIRST OF ALL, LET ME ASSERT MY FIRM BELIEF THAT THE ONLY THING WE HAVE TO FEAR IS... FEAR ITSELF — NAMELESS, UNREASONING, UNJUSTIFIED TERROR WHICH PARALYSES NEEDED EFFORTS TO CONVERT RETREAT INTO ADVANCE."

US President Franklin D Roosevelt in his inaugural address, 1933.

★ HELPING THE NEEDY

The New Deal reforms in the USA brought electricity to millions of homes and built much of the infrastructure that is still in use today. It also marked a radical change in social policy, which laid the framework for the USA's welfare state. Other countries extended their welfare system, with Britain beginning to lay the foundations that would lead to a 'cradle to grave' social security system as implemented after World War II.

US women work on military aircraft during the the rapid industrialisation that began at the outbreak of World War II.

A poster advertises New York City's land and water airports built in the 1930s and 1940s.

GLOSSARY

appeasement
Making concessions to avoid a war. In the 1930s, Britain followed a policy of appeasement with Germany .

bank run
When a large number of people try to withdraw their money from a bank at once.

boom and bust
A type of economic cycle that sees huge growth followed by a slump or depression.

bread line
A line of people waiting to receive food.

dust bowl
An area of Kansas, northern Texas and Oklahoma in the USA affected by severe dust storms caused by soil erosion during the Great Depression.

fascism
A state ruled by one person or party that attempts to impose military discipline on society at the expense of individual freedom.

federal
A system of government in which states form a unity but remain independent in internal affairs. In the USA, federal relates to the central US government.

gold standard
The system in which the value of a country's currency is defined in terms of gold, and which can be exchanged for gold at fixed rates.

interest
Money that is charged by a bank for borrowing money or money that you earn from keeping your money in a bank.

mortgage
A loan given to a person to buy property. If the borrower fails to pay back the loan, the lender can take possession of the property or sell it.

New Deal
A series of economic reforms and public works programmes introduced by US president Franklin D Roosevelt to tackle the effects of the Great Depression.

protectionism
Protecting a country's economy by limiting imported goods from other countries and placing tariffs, or taxes, on them.

rearmament
Acquiring or building up a new supply of weapons in readiness for war.

reparation payments
Compensation payments made by a defeated nation, such as Germany, to pay for war damage.

stocks
Shares in the value of a particular company or industry.

stock exchange
A system or place where stocks (see above) and bonds (an agreement to lend money to a company) are bought and sold.

speculation
Investing in financial transactions with the hope of future profit but with the risk of considerable loss.

tariffs
A tax or duty paid on an import (bringing a product into the country) or export (sending a product to another country).

taxes
Money payable on a person's income, a product, service or financial transaction, which contributes to the government's revenue.

totalitarianism
When a state is ruled by one leader or party seeking to control all aspects of life.

trade union
An organised association of people, often in a trade or business, formed to protect their working rights and interests.

FURTHER INFORMATION

★ BOOKS TO READ

History of the World
Plantagenet Somerset Fry
Dorling Kindersley 2007
A definitive world history for children,
from the time when humans first walked
the Earth to the age of space travel.

Oxford Children's History of the World
Neil Grant
Oxford University Press 2006
An illustrated book on the whole of human
history, beginning with ancient times and
ending with the world today.

**Aspects of European
History – 1789–1980**
Stephen J Lee
Routledge 1988
Examines the most common topics
in European history in a clear and
digestible way.

★ MUSEUMS AND WEBSITES TO VISIT

BBC Bitesize
www.bbc.co.uk/education/topics/zsr782p
Includes information and a film about the
Wall Street Crash and the Great Depression,
testimonies from people who lived during
the Depression and photographs of
migrant farmers.

Encyclopedia Britannica
www.britannica.com
Online encyclopedia for children
ages 6–10 and 11–14.